Catherine Ayres

Janus

Indigo Dreams Publishing

First Edition: Janus
First published in Great Britain in 2024 by:
Indigo Dreams Publishing
24, Forest Houses
Cookworthy Moor
Halwill
Beaworthy
Devon
EX21 5UU

www.indigodreamspublishing.com

ISBN 978-1-912876-89-1

British Library Cataloguing in Publication Data. A CIP record for this book can be obtained from the British Library.

Designed and typeset in Palatino Linotype by Indigo Dreams. Cover artwork/design by Ronnie Goodyer based on an original painting by Vilhelm Hammershøi. ©2024 Ronnie Goodyer

Printed and bound in Great Britain by 4edge Ltd.

Papers used by Indigo Dreams are recyclable products made from wood grown in sustainable forests following the guidance of the Forest Stewardship Council.

For my family, who travels with me.

Acknowledgements

Grateful thanks go to the following publications where these poems, or earlier versions of them, have appeared:
Ambit, The Northern Correspondent, Ink, Sweat and Tears, Domestic Cherry, The Lampeter Review, Proletarian Poetry, Write Where We Are Now, The Fat Damsel, The Emma Press Anthology of Love ed. Rachel Piercey (The Emma Press, 2018), *Writing Motherhood: A Creative Anthology* ed. Carolyn Jess-Cooke (Seren, 2017), *A Bee's Breakfast* (Beautiful Dragon Collaborations), *Noble Dissent* (Beautiful Dragon Collaborations), *A Hut a Byens* (Bamburgh Heritage Trust, 2022), *Storm Brain: The Hippocrates Book of the Brain* eds. Wendy French, Michael Hulse, Donald Singer (Hippocrates Press, 2021). 'Travelling' was displayed on the Tyne and Wear Metro as part of Poetry in Motion; 'To Disappointment: An Assay' placed 3rd in Ambit's poetry competition, 2014; 'Oddbods' was a finalist in the Live Canon competition, 2016. 'Four Corners' was made into a poetry film by Manchester Metropolitan University.

Also by Catherine Ayres

Amazon, IDP, 2016.

Dark Matter 5 – poems by Catherine Ayres and Steve Urwin, Black Light Engine Room Press, 2015.

CONTENTS

CONTENTS

Janus

'Forward I look, and backward, and below
I count, as god of avenues and gates,
The years that through my portals come and go.'

~ from 'January' by Henry Wadsworth Longfellow

January 2015 – a new sofa arrives

Janus

What might never happen, did.
My heart's a holloway, a healed wound
but January's naked on the lawn –
the cat dies, the car dies, there's flu –
and so I carry on. Halfway through,
the sofa shuffles out into the snow,
winces like a hermit in the light,
lets two lads coax its bulk into a van.
I see it go, sit cross-legged on the floor,
a space where I have nursed and fucked, slept
chemo off and watched a husband leave.
The clock ticks loud inside this shallow grave,
this square of sun that wasn't there before.

January 2012 – travelling to Allenheads

Travelling

Piebald fell
setting its flank against the twilight.

I can feel its fervour, its reassurance,
warm breath against cold air.

I'm travelling towards love.

This magnificence will soon be held in
a cup, a kiss, a candle

and my heart will contain what can't be contained
on this lonely road.

February 2014 – a trip to Edinburgh to see the Louise Bourgeois exhibition

Spider

A woman weaves her body into art
Her secrets are a thread she must unpick
The present holds the past inside its heart

A woman spools until her silk is thick
Caught in the twisting spiral is despair
Her secrets are a thread she must unpick

A woman's life is not beyond repair
The morning circles through a metronome
Caught in the twisting spiral is despair

A woman hangs lost objects in her home
She traps their silence in a fragile cage
The morning circles through a metronome

A woman fills the blankness of a page
Her spinning wheels give everything away
She traps their silence in a fragile cage

The day invades the night, invades the day
A woman weaves her body into art
Her spinning wheels give everything away

The present holds the past inside its heart

The first line of the last stanza taken from Louise Bourgeois, Diary, 7th February 1995, 'Has the day invaded the night or the night invaded the day?'

'Her spinning wheels give everything away' is a reference to 'I give everything away', 2010, her series of six large-format hand-coloured etchings.

February 2009 – observing my neighbour

Ignoring Alicia

If I were you
I'd be a piss-take
a walk of shame down this quiet street
a *What the fuck?* in an empty afternoon.

If I were you
I'd have swollen mouth eyes
a flick-knife fringe
a temper as tight as a rubber band ball.

If I were you
I'd hold court in my backyard
rail against a shadow
on my doorstep throne
the street light fawning over me.

If I were you
I'd be a dragon
wear a dress like scaled skin
crawl through smashed glass at midnight
let the copper cut his eyeballs
on the sharp edge of my arse.

If I were you
I'd get a job
pick the last of the scabs off a clean life
flutter my blinds like a pang

when what I used to be
rollercoasters round the bend
saluting the woman
who's pretending not to look.

March 2020 – lockdown declared by UK government

Tonight

the stars aren't enough, or the Sainsbury's
sign, or the empty forecourt, floating
in space. Streetlights weep like snowdrops,
a beech hedge sings in a trickle of wind.
No moon. Its face would not be enough,
even now, when silence aches in my head,
across this town, the moor, and further out
into a darkness we can't see, despite
the fear and the searching, the telescopes
in our chests, every news report a dropped pin
on the library floor of our lives.

Spring dusk.
  Blossom hangs
 its tiny lights.

March 2020 – lockdown

Four corners

The irony of spring and its tiny fingers, of lapwings,
rain showers, diamonds on the pane, the irony of light
through cloud, through curtains, through speckles
in an eye, the irony of postcards, the time it took to frame
them, of dusting, bin day, of a short walk to see the trees,
the irony of my favourite oak, how its shadow spreads,
the irony of chips and teatime and tomato sauce, the irony
of the earth's four corners and its horsemen, leaping out
as the sermon drones on, my choirgirl's ruff suddenly tight,
and afterwards, in the graveyard, of my dad, strong and handsome,
aged 40, telling me *it's just a story, everything's going to be alright.*

April 2020 – lockdown

Mum

When I crunch down your drive
with some carrots, a wholemeal loaf –
unsliced – you stand in the garage
and use the remote to tilt its door

emerging slowly, feet first,
like a breech birth, or Darth Vader,
if Darth Vader wore Skechers, a John Lewis
top. For a moment, your face floats

then you step forward, submissive,
as if these groceries were the Host,
and I step back, as if your eyes
were metre rules. We're silent,

ceremonious, a bit pissed off. Mum,
we're more alike than I let on.
Behind you, in the kitchen,
there's an awkward hug. Cheese scones.

April 2006 – Easter

This is not a holy verse

'The first day of the week cometh Mary Magdalene early, when it was yet dark, unto the sepulchre…' – John 20:1

Early, early,
in the cage between stars and dawn,
she startles awake,
half dreaming,
still livid with dreams.

How can her brothers lie with sorrow
in this hollow light?

Streets line the city's palm.
She fills them with echoes and dust.

At the gate, walls unravel into scrub.
A soldier barks.
The first bird sings.

There's a storm in her head,
there is thunder and blood.

The garden does not speak.
Its speckled tongues are silent,
each leaf cups an unsaid prayer.

Morning splits, candle-soft,
and her eyes meet the secret of the tomb,
the great stone rolled, the great stone
frail as a wing in rising light.

What did she want?
Not his empty clothes,
the memory of his shape in the dark.

This is not a holy verse.
But I have knelt at the cross,
I have loved a man.

May 2020 – weeding the front garden

Ground Elder

If
I don't
let my mind

wander
out of
its neat borders

spring
will continue
to be beautiful.

Look!
Buds form
on the lilac

Grandma
gave me
before her thoughts

escaped.
Ground Elder
refuses to leave.

Best
to weed
my garden slowly

work
the trowel
under its roots.

How
do you
die? she said.

May 2009 – a confrontation with my neighbour

Kyle's dad berates a group of boys in my back garden

Divvent ye think I divvent knaa what's been gan on doon that back lane the day, mind. Divvent get us wrang, bairns ull be bairns and we've aal hoyed some clemmies in wa time, like, and ah knaa he can be a little shite – sorry, hen, you been a school teacher an that – but haway, man! He's littler than aal of yus put together and naeone desorves the size of egg borstin on his heed. Canny clip! And afore ye start blubberin Tyler, just mind that your lot's from the same place as mine. Aye, ya mam's nana and wor nana bided beside each other up the tree streets – canniest wife yu'd eva meet, tegs like a bornt oot village, mind, how. So watch it, right? Or ah'll have to knack the lot of yus. Cheers, pet. And Tyler, tell ya fither to get yu a proper footy short the morn. Naeone likes a mackem. Fuckin disgrace, son.

hoyed – thrown   *clemmies – stones*
tegs – teeth   *short – shirt*
canny clip – what a state *the morn – tomorrow*
mackem – someone from Sunderland

June 1983 – a weekend playing out with my best friend Emma

Oddbods

We embroider our edges with slow smiles,
tuck ourselves into home-made jumpers
and hide in our mothers' expectations.
We are happiest in the avocado shadow of bathrooms,
turning over sea urchins with trembling hands;
or crouched next to French windows, listening
to a scratched recording of birdsong.
Our guinea pigs are called Monica - they are both boys.
We like our eggs hard boiled, our celery lined with salt.
We *know* how to use a soup spoon.
We do not understand posters; all our clippings
are pinned to floral wallpaper. Our bedrooms
are like conches, delicate and full of whispers.
(It is often hard to leave them).
Laughter clatters round us like knives falling in another room;
we are soft and solemn as Sundays and do not flinch.
One day we will live in the tree on the hill,
hang our horse brasses from its branches.
When our dandelion clocks swim like spiders
towards the moon, we will teach the teddies about Jesus,
serenade the cowpats with our favourite hymns.
It won't matter that our dollies are lonely;
we will draw them close, wipe the tears
from their large, unblinking eyes.

June 2016 – Brexit referendum

Don't leave

the dandelion growing through concrete
the broken windows birthing stars
the puddles magicking their rainbows
the new skin smiling under scars

the tags shouting loud in the underpass
the pigeon shitting on spikes
the friends still alive in photographs
the dust furring slants of light

the street lamp stuttering at twilight
the plastic bag roosting with the crows
the back lane cradling its secrets
the old song rising in your throat

the dead leaves dancing on the forecourt
the flyers bleeding in the rain
the motorway howling in the darkness:
remain, remain, remain

July 2015 – a holiday in Brighton

Not quite déjà-vu

Ascending the water ride
I suddenly remember Leith,
the four of us pissed and maudlin,
conversation fading into sleep
until Alec drains his glass,
tells Michelle she's all that matters,
his cheeks flushed as an open heart
and you say 'You're so lucky'
then stop, look away before I understand.
Sometimes memories make circles,
glint like birds in the light;
plummeting now, eyes blurred,
I think of your face,
how my stomach lurched.

July 2017 – swimming in Coniston Water

Two sons in a lake

Their bodies rise
from water into sky,

out of context in blue.
My little monoliths,

the camera's turned you to stone
and I search the space between us.

Youngest faces me,
his torso full of sun;

our ripples overlap, like soundwaves,
two notes in the same song.

Oldest boy is further out;
did I ask him, or did he decide

to stand on the point of turning
new shadows on his chest?

I want to swim back into shot
so our circles touch.

Behind him, distant pine,
the mountain in its own light.

August 2017 – visiting LA

Luxury spa, California

At the spa,
the waitress stands very straight.
She swivels her head before she sees me,
her smile is wide but tight.
The pool is salt water.
There are rows of recliners,
each with a fitted towel.
The parasols are midnight blue;
to leave their shade is to submit,
to be split open by light,
the sky almost white,
a distant eagle frail as a wasp.

The waiter walks travellator-smooth.
He brings a silver tray,
feeds me enchiladas, frozen grapes.
All afternoon I play the baby bird:
I say *Thank you*, he says *Of course.*

Dinner is served at dusk.
A chalk board says 'Pink Moment 7:48'.
I glimpse the sunset through champagne flutes,
we eat under the stars.

In the restroom mirror I am moth-pale,
false eyes, an ordinary dress.
I paint my lips for a long time.

Next morning, we drive to the sea.
Nodding donkeys work the scrub,
palm trees lurch and glitter.
A trailer park squats in the heat;
there are wind chimes, nasturtiums,
suddenly a paddock full of foals.

I watch them circle the dust,
imagine the thrum of hooves,
a pulse.

August 2023 – Remembering A Level results day, 1991

To Disappointment: An Assay
(after Jane Hirshfield's 'To Spareness: An Assay')

You stumble towards Sadness
but are pulled back by the sticky hands of Optimism.

You are often a mountain reflected in a puddle,
or a fish eye glimpsed in a lake,
but never a whale thrashing in a swimming pool.

Your dimension is a small, sudden decline,
an unseen kerb to the distracted cyclist.

Thinking of you, I picture
spoons, car parks, cat sick.
Tampons are always a disappointment.

You are present
in geography teachers, Bedlington terriers and tugboats.

All tombolas whisper your name.

Your song is "My Funny Valentine".
Your vegetable, a sprout.

Your colour is not the bruised grey of a pregnant rain cloud
but the faded grey of a rain-spattered postcard
left on the windowsill of a holiday home in Skegness.

Your season is the last week of August.

You are immune to accumulation,
each of your hillocks clearly separated by
thick ribbons of dirty dishwater.

You are the woman wearing an A-line skirt in a meeting,
who could so easily prise herself apart, but instead
washes her eyes in the strip lights,
holding small weights of silence
in her tightly clasped hands.

September 2013 – walking to the Staiths

At Dunston Staiths

For eighty years it was an open vein,
bleeding coal into the Tyne.
A village before the new-builds sprouted,
the staiths' wooden spine slinked
between ships; use not ornament,
this ancient monument a means to an end.

It's quiet now. Joggers dot the waggons'
old route; commuters left hours ago.
The bloke in the café sighs.
Someone's set fire to the restoration,
tagged carefully sourced wood.
Kids fuck under the new slats.
A dirty protest? Boredom more like.

We look out at the lagoon.
It's eerie, fat with silt,
made strange with curlew cries.
I squint at them, these little dredgers,
balancing on what's left.

September 2016 – Rothbury

Dove Crag

On the ridge, startled light.
Pines brood in their slants,
the river glistens like a kill.
I hover over a small life,
search for its sparks
in a sinew of land.
I burned down years ago,
speckled flares between hill and sea,
tiny fires in closed rooms,
all my hiding places.
The grouse shouts 'Go back!'
but I'm nearer the moon
than these tangled maps,
its feathered face
ash flecks in blue.

October 2019 – diagnosed with breast cancer for the second time

October is Breast Cancer Awareness month

and the letter says
there is something
on the mammogram
and the MRI.

That night
I look in the mirror.
My single breast hangs its head
like a lonely twin.

    *

In the recall room
we're forced to wear
dusty pink.
I scan a magazine;
the newbies skim-read fear.

    *

On the ultrasound
my flesh swirls
like the feathers
of an owl's face.

Your breast tissue is still dense
but can you see this string?

    *

I'm lying sideways
nipple clamped and numb.
The needle flicks its tongue.

I chat to the nurse
while she stems the blood.
Afterwards my mum takes me for lunch.

*

The surgeon draws circles in red pen.
These are normal cells.
She fills them with spirals.
My faulty gene is a toddler
who colours outside the lines.

*

She sighs.
You're young
to have no breasts.
And slim!
Not enough fat
to make new ones.

*

My son was six the first time.
He said: *Mummy,*
will it grow back?
Now the teen asks:
Where do they put it?
In the bin?

*

It's Halloween.
Tonight I will come home
with freshly-painted seams
and sit in a costume
I can't take off.

October 2019 – walking to the castle

Dunstanburgh

You squat on the horizon's line
like a lost crown, a last resort.

To reach you I must balance tipped
land with sea that stretches half the sky –

you wait. The basalt beach is black
with tide; it splays a fossil wing towards

your shore and there is no turning back
from your wind-sucked gate, the grimace

of its antlered mask, the south wall's snake
to St. Margaret's cove, foam a swan's neck in the swell.

I love your edge and absence, how screaming cliffs
enclose the altar of your empty rooms,

how treason echoes in the scurvy grass
where swallows dip and play. A crow hoists

its wings on a string of wind, floats away
across the ghost land of your meres.

Your towers clutch the air like drowning
hands, flags and fires gone. Still here.

November 2018 – thinking of a friend who's sad

When I say I think about you every day

I mean your heart's small particulars,
its stitches, I'm pressing them to mine,
I mean your eyelashes, I'm kissing them
with blinks, I mean our backs are blessed
at our kitchen sinks when we slump in a slant
of light we can't see, I mean our fingertips
leave moons on the glass, I mean the white horse,
the liquid deer, I mean sometimes I fold into an owl
and scalp our furred hearts clean, I mean look up,
you're luminous.

November 2021 – visiting the ossuary at St Aidan's church, Bamburgh

The Irish Girl (Skeleton 73)

Because you strung a line
from Ireland
to the northern seat
      of a sainted king
and spent your short life
   at the loom,
fingers spread
    through warp and woof
I will call you *wæfer-ganger*
            walker-weaver
                spider.

Such thin strands
    to spin into a life:
you were tall,
      strong-thighed,
your front tooth
    held a needle's groove;
I want to know the colour
     of your eyes,
  the shape of your laugh
    in a spring tide's storm,
  how you prayed

and if somehow you know
   that your bones
   have left the earth-bowl
in which you bathed
    for centuries – hugging
yourself, head facing west –
   to shimmer like pins
in a zinc box, blessed

        by villagers
who share your faith.
        Little spider,

your web
        has stretched
                into strange times
where everything has changed;
but geese still drop
        a stitch
                into bare sky
and above the crypt
        Christ streams
                through a stained-glass face.
So sleep now. You're safe.

'This young woman was probably a weaver or needle-worker for the royal court. The nick in her front teeth may have come from holding the threads in her mouth as she worked' – information taken from https://bamburghbones.org/ossuary-entry/baec-bord/

December 2011 – remembering Christmas 1986

Snow

Midnight. Absence beyond the glass.
I step outside into an empty world,
forty years washed clean,
to find I'm walking with my father
towards the chapel's clank,
the field a feather,
breath furry in the dark.

Inside, candles wobble on their stalks,
the organ splits, a village sings.
I leave two heads in flickered light,
a young man and his daughter,
pressed like a foal against his flank,

swirl back to the sleeping house,
my children, the door's bright edge.
The moon waits, open-mouthed.
By dawn, all paths will be lost.

December 2014 – Christmas Eve alone

The single woman and the lights

They're bunched in the bag like an addled brain.
Last Christmas it was easy: he shook them free,
or maybe it was the mulled wine, the thought of his hands.
Now each strung head is desperate, locked in a final kiss.
I spider them apart, an afternoon lost to unpicking,
set them straight as graves on the living room floor.
It's dusk. I take them in my arms and we slow dance
round the tree. When they wince through the tinsel
my eyes swell. These plucky buds. Another year.

Indigo Dreams Publishing Ltd
24, Forest Houses
Cookworthy Moor
Halwill
Beaworthy
Devon
EX21 5UU
www.indigodreamspublishing.com